Published exclusively by
Saint Benedict Press
in association with
Creations for Children International, Belgium
All rights reserved

Illustrations, concept and artwork © A. M. Lefèvre, M. Loiseaux,
M. Nathan-Deiller, A. Van Gool.
First published and produced by
Creations for Children International, Belgium. www.c4ci.com
All rights reserved

Introductory Letter by
Father Benedict Groeschel, C.F.R.
copyright © 2012 Saint Benedict Press
Charlotte, NC USA
All rights reserved

New Testament Bible Story text
edited and adapted by Sarah Laurell
copyright © 2012 Saint Benedict Press
Charlotte, NC USA
All rights reserved

Printed in China

www.SaintBenedictPress.com

SAINT BENEDICT✝PRESS

$\mathcal{M}$Y
$\mathcal{F}$IRST $\mathcal{C}$OMMUNION
$\mathcal{B}$IBLE

PRESENTED TO

Avry Robinson

ON

May 11, 2013

BY

Rev Lous R. Palmieri

Dear Child,

Today is a very special day. Your whole family is filled with happiness for you, and so am I. We are happy because you will be given a great gift today, one that is better than anything you could get on your birthday or even on Christmas. You will be given the gift of meeting Jesus in a very special way.

I know that you have learned who Jesus is. Your parents and teachers have taught you that He is the Son of God, the Second Person of the Blessed Trinity. They have told you that Jesus became a human being just like you and me. Jesus even died for us, so that we can live forever with Him in Heaven.

Do you know why Jesus did that? It is because He loves us. He loves you, and He loves me. He loves your mother and your father and all your friends. He loves everybody, even the people we don't love. Jesus loves us so much that He wants to be as close to us as possible. That's why He gave us the gift you will receive today. This gift is Jesus Himself, and it is called Holy Communion.

Every Sunday you go to Mass with your family, and you see the priest consecrate bread and wine. When the

priest does that, the bread and wine become Jesus. They become His Body and Blood. Today when the priest gives you Holy Communion, it may seem like ordinary bread, but it is not. It is really and truly Jesus. Today Jesus will come into your heart and soul. When you receive Holy Communion, He will be closer to you than anyone else ever could be.

Many years ago, before you were born and even before your parents were born I received this wonderful gift for the first time. I was just your age, and I was dressed in my best clothes, just as you are now. I knelt before the priest with all the boys and girls in my class and I received Jesus in Holy Communion.

I remember how close to Him I felt, and I remember how I wanted to thank Him for coming to me in this special way. I wanted to be very, very good so that each time Jesus came to my heart and soul He would see that I loved Him as much as He loved me.

I have received Holy Communion many, many times since then, but I will never forget my first Holy Communion. I pray that you will love Jesus forever, and I pray that you will let Him come into your heart and soul many, many times.

—Fr. Benedict Groeschel, C.F.R.

THE ANNUNCIATION

During King Herod's reign, a young woman lived in Galilee, in the town of Nazareth. Her name was Mary and she was betrothed to a carpenter called Joseph. One day God sent the angel Gabriel to Mary.

"Hail, full of grace, the Lord is with you!" he said. "Do not be afraid, Mary, for you have found favor with God. Behold, you will bear a son, whom you will name Jesus. He will be great and will be called the Son of the Most High. His kingdom will have no end."

"How can this be," asked Mary, "since I am a virgin?" And the angel told her, "The Holy Spirit shall come upon you and the power of the Most High will overshadow you. Your child will be holy, the Son of God." Mary bowed her head. "Behold, I am the handmaid of the Lord," she replied. "Let it be done to me according to your word."

(Luke 1:26–38)

THE NATIVITY

The most powerful ruler in all the land was Augustus, the Roman Emperor. Augustus wanted to know how many of his subjects lived in each country. He ordered each person to return to the town of his birth so he could count everyone in a census.

Joseph and Mary traveled to Bethlehem. When they arrived, all of the inns were full. They had to stay in a stable where Jesus was born. Mary wrapped him in swaddling clothes and laid him in a manger.

That night, an angel of the Lord appeared to a group of shepherds watching their flocks in the fields. "Do not be afraid, I bring you good news of great joy," he said. "Today, a savior has been born for you. He is Christ the Lord. You will find him in a stable, lying in a manger. Glory to God in the highest!" The shepherds went and found the baby Jesus in his manger.

(Luke 2:1–20)

THE VISIT OF THE MAGI

Far away in the East, wise men called magi had seen a new star in the heavens. They followed the star to Jerusalem and came before King Herod.

"Where is the newborn King of the Jews?" they asked Herod. "We have come to worship him." The chief priests and scribes told Herod about a prophecy that said the King of the Jews would be born in Bethlehem. Herod was troubled and asked the magi to send word when they had found the child. "For I wish to honor him myself," he said.

The magi continued following the star until it stopped over the place where Jesus was. They entered the house and found Jesus with his mother Mary. The magi fell to the ground and worshiped him. They opened their treasures and gave Jesus precious gifts of gold, frankincense and myrrh. In a dream the magi were warned not to return to Herod. So they went back to their country by another way.

(Matthew 2:1–12)

14

THE FLIGHT INTO EGYPT

After the wise men left, the angel of the Lord appeared to Joseph in a dream. "Wake up," he commanded. "Take Jesus and his mother and flee to Egypt. Stay there until I tell you." The angel explained, "Herod is going to search for the child to destroy him." Joseph took his family and left Bethlehem that same night.

When Herod saw that the wise men had tricked him, he was furious. He ordered his soldiers to go to Bethlehem and the surrounding area and kill all the boys who were under two years of age. After Herod died, the angel of the Lord appeared in a dream to Joseph in Egypt.

"Rise, take Jesus and his mother and return to Israel," the angel said, "for those who wanted to kill him are dead." Joseph obeyed the angel. He, Mary, and Jesus returned to Israel and lived in the town of Nazareth.

(Matthew 2:13–22)

FINDING THE CHILD JESUS IN THE TEMPLE

When Jesus was twelve years old, he went with his parents to Jerusalem for the feast of Passover. After the feast was over, Joseph and Mary travelled toward home for a day before they looked for Jesus. They thought he was with their friends and relatives.

When they could not find him, Joseph and Mary returned to Jerusalem. After three days they found Jesus in the temple. He was sitting among the teachers, listening to them and asking them questions. All who heard Jesus were amazed by his understanding and his answers.

"Son, why have you done this to us? Your father and I have been looking for you anxiously," Mary exclaimed.

Jesus answered, "Why were you looking for me? Did you not know that I must be in my Father's house?" Mary and Joseph did not understand what he meant. Jesus returned to Nazareth and was obedient to them. Mary kept all these things that happened in her heart and Jesus advanced in wisdom as he grew.

(Luke 2:41–52)

19

THE BAPTISM OF JESUS IN THE RIVER JORDAN

When Jesus was about thirty years old, he went to the River Jordan where John the Baptist was preaching and baptizing people. When John saw Jesus, he proclaimed, "Behold, the Lamb of God, who takes away the sins of the world! He is mightier than I am. I am not worthy to unfasten the strap on his sandals. I use water, but he will baptize you with the Holy Spirit and with fire."

Jesus asked John to baptize him, but John said, "I need to be baptized by you, why do you come to me?" Jesus answered him, "Allow it for now, for by doing this we fulfill all righteousness." After Jesus was baptized, the heavens opened and the Holy Spirit descended on him like a dove. Everyone heard God's voice say: "This is my beloved Son, with whom I am well pleased." John the Baptist saw this and said, "I have seen and have borne witness that this is the Son of God."

(Matthew 3:1–17; Mark 1:1–11; Luke 3:1–23; John 1:19–34)

THE TWELVE APOSTLES

Jesus traveled to Galilee to preach the good news of God. Wherever he went, crowds gathered to hear him preach. "The time is fulfilled and the Kingdom of God is at hand," he told them. "Repent of your sins and believe in the gospel."

One day, Jesus passed two fishermen, Simon, also called Peter, and his brother Andrew. "Leave your nets and follow me," Jesus told them. "I will make you fishers of men." Peter and Andrew did as Jesus asked and became his first disciples. Jesus also found two other fishermen, James and John, and called them to join him. The next day, Jesus called Philip. Then he called Matthew, the tax collector.

Jesus gathered all of his disciples around him. He named twelve apostles to preach the gospel and gave them the power to cast out demons and heal the sick. These twelve were Peter, his brother Andrew, James, his brother John, Philip, Matthew, Bartholomew, Thomas, James, Thaddeus, Simon, and Judas Iscariot.

(Matthew 4:17–22, 9:9, 10:1–4; Mark 1:14–20, 2:13–14, 3:13–19; Luke 5:1–11, 5:27–28, 6:12–16; John 1:35–43)

THE WEDDING AT CANA

There was a wedding in the town of Cana and Mary, Jesus' mother, was there. Jesus and his apostles were also invited. After some time Mary saw that all the wine had been consumed. She told Jesus, "They have no wine."

At first, Jesus said, "Woman, what is that to me and you? My hour has not yet come." But Mary was full of faith and said to the servants, "Do whatever he tells you." Jesus had the servants fill six large jars with water. "Now draw some out and take it to the steward of the feast."

Without knowing where it came from, the steward tasted the cup the servants brought to him. He said to the bridegroom, "Everyone serves the best wine first and saves the cheaper wine until the guests have drunk too much. But you have served your best wine last."

This was the first miracle that Jesus performed. It revealed his glory, and his apostles began to believe in him.

(John 2:1–11)

THE SERMON ON THE MOUNT

Jesus and his apostles traveled the country, preaching the gospel of the Kingdom of God. When Jesus saw a great crowd following him, he went up a mountain and sat down to teach them.

He said, "Blessed are the pure of heart, for they will see God. Blessed are the peacemakers, for they will be children of God. Blessed are they who are persecuted for my sake, for theirs is the kingdom of heaven.

"Love your enemies and do good to those who hurt you. Give to others and expect nothing in return. Be merciful as God is merciful. Forgive and you will be forgiven."

Jesus also taught them to pray: "Our Father who art in heaven, hallowed be thy name. Thy kingdom come, thy will be done, on earth as it is in heaven. Give us this day our daily bread; and forgive us our trespasses, as we forgive those who trespass against us, and lead us not into temptation, but deliver us from evil."

(Matthew 5:1–12; Luke 6:20–49)

THE PARABLE OF THE PRODIGAL SON

Jesus often taught using stories called parables. Once, people were complaining because he visited with sinners. Jesus said, "All the angels rejoice when just one sinner repents."

Jesus continued with this parable. "A man had two sons. The younger son asked for half of his father's wealth and then wasted all of it partying. When a famine struck, the son had nothing to eat, not even animal slops. Finally, he decided to go home and humbly beg for his father's forgiveness. But while he was on the road, his father caught sight of him.

"He ran to his son, embraced him, and planned a huge feast. The older brother was angry because he was good all the time and had never had a party. His father explained, 'My son, you are always with me and everything I have is yours. We are celebrating because your brother was dead and is alive again; he was lost and has been found.'"

(Luke 15:10–32)

28

THE PARABLE OF THE GOOD SAMARITAN

One day while Jesus was preaching, a lawyer stood up and questioned him. "The law says that we should love our neighbor as ourselves," said the lawyer. "But who is my neighbor?"

In reply Jesus said, "A man was traveling to Jerusalem when robbers attacked him and left him for dead. A priest and a Levite who should have followed the law saw the man, but they did nothing to help him. Instead they crossed to the other side of the road and passed him by.

"But then a Samaritan came by," said Jesus. "He helped the man, treated his wounds, and took him to an inn to recover. The next day he had to leave, but he gave the innkeeper money to look after the injured man."

Jesus asked the lawyer, "Which of these men was a neighbor to the robbers' victim?" And the lawyer replied, "The man who treated him with mercy." Jesus said, "Go and do likewise."

(Luke 10:25–37)

THE PARABLE OF THE SOWER

On another occasion, Jesus told this parable:
"A farmer went out to sow his seed. Some of it fell on the path and birds ate it. Some of the seed fell on rocky ground where it withered because it didn't have enough water. Some fell among thorns which grew with it and choked it. And some seed fell onto good soil and produced an abundant harvest."

The apostles asked Jesus what his story meant. Jesus said, "The seed is the word of God. The seed on the path represents people who hear the word but they allow the devil to steal their belief. The people who are like the rocky ground receive the word joyfully, but they have no depth and their belief fails when it is tested. The thorns are like people whose faith is choked by the cares of the world. But the good soil represents people who hear the word, embrace it, and bear fruit through perseverance."

(Matthew 13:3–9, 13:18–23; Luke 8:4–15)

JESUS HEALS THE SICK

One day some men brought their paralyzed friend to see Jesus. There was such a crowd around Jesus that the men climbed onto the roof and lowered their friend into the room below.

When Jesus saw their faith he said, "Friend, your sins are forgiven." The scribes and chief priests were shocked. "Only God can forgive sins!" Jesus asked, "Is it easier to say 'Your sins are forgiven,' or 'Rise and walk?' But so that you may know that I can forgive sins," he said to the paralyzed man, "Rise, take your mat, and go home." The man stood up immediately, picked up his mat, and went home glorifying God.

Another time a Roman soldier asked Jesus to heal his dying servant. "I will come to him," said Jesus. But the soldier replied, "Lord, I am not worthy to have you come under my roof; but only say the word, and my servant will be healed." Jesus marveled and said, "No one in Israel has faith like yours." And the servant was healed from that very moment.

(Luke 5:17–26; Matthew 8:5 13)

JESUS WALKS ON WATER

After preaching for three days, Jesus went to pray by himself. The apostles wanted to sail to the other side of a lake, but while they were in the boat a strong wind began to blow. Suddenly they saw Jesus walking towards them across the water. They were terrified and thought he was a ghost.

But Jesus said, "Take courage! It is I, do not be afraid." Peter said, "If it is you Lord, command me to come to you on the water." Jesus said, "Come." Peter got out of the boat and began to walk on the water toward Jesus. But when he saw how strong the wind was and how high the waves were, Peter became afraid and started to sink.

He cried out, "Lord, save me!" Jesus immediately grasped Peter's hand and caught him. When they got back into the boat, the wind stopped blowing. The apostles in the boat worshipped Jesus and said, "Truly you are the Son of God."

(Matthew 14:22–33; Mark 6:45–52; John 6:16–21)

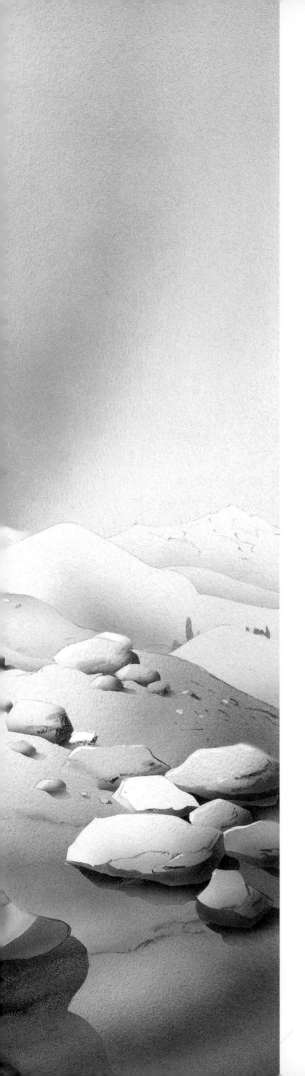

THE TRANSFIGURATION

Jesus taught his apostles saying, "Whoever wants to follow me must deny himself and take up his cross daily." Then, he took Peter, James, and John with him up a mountain to pray. At the top of the mountain, Jesus was transfigured. His face shone like the sun and his clothes became as white as light.

Elijah and Moses appeared next to Jesus and were speaking with him. Then, a bright cloud cast a shadow over them. A voice came from the cloud and said, "This is my beloved Son, with whom I am well pleased; listen to him."

When the apostles heard the voice, they were terrified and fell to the ground. But Jesus came and touched them and said, "Rise and do not be afraid." When the apostles stood up, Jesus was alone. As they were coming down the mountain, Jesus said, "Keep this vision a secret until I am raised from the dead." (Matthew 17:1–9; Mark 9:2–9; Luke 9:28–36)

JESUS AND THE CHILDREN

Wherever Jesus went, parents brought their children and babies for him to touch and bless. Little children gathered around him as he preached, all trying to get as close to him as they could.

The apostles thought the parents and children were bothering Jesus by crowding him. But when Jesus saw the apostles trying to chase the children away, he called the children to himself. Jesus said, "Let the little children come to me and do not hinder them. The Kingdom of God belongs to such as these."

Jesus pointed to the small children playing at his feet. "You should all be more like these children," he said to the listening crowd. "Truly I say to you, whoever does not receive the Kingdom of God with the trust of a child will not enter it." Then Jesus embraced the children, placed his hands on them, and blessed them.

(Matthew 19:13–15; Mark 10:13–16; Luke 18:15–17)

LAZARUS COMES BACK TO LIFE

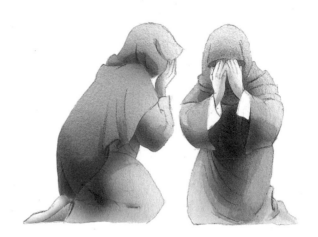

Lazarus, a friend of Jesus, was dying. His sisters, Mary and Martha, sent word to Jesus that Lazarus was ill. But Jesus said, "Lazarus is sick so that I might be glorified by means of it." After two days, Jesus told his apostles that Lazarus had died and said, "Let us go to him."

Martha and Mary came to meet Jesus. "Lord, if you had been with him when he was first ill," they sobbed, "he would have been healed." When Jesus saw how sad they were, he also wept. Then they took Jesus to the tomb where Lazarus had been buried.

"Roll away the stone that covers the entrance," Jesus told them. He looked up towards heaven. "Thank you Father, I know you have always heard my prayers. Now let everyone see that I do your will." Jesus faced the tomb and cried, "Lazarus, come out!" With joy and amazement, the people watched as Lazarus walked out of the tomb.

(John 11:1–44)

JESUS ENTERS JERUSALEM

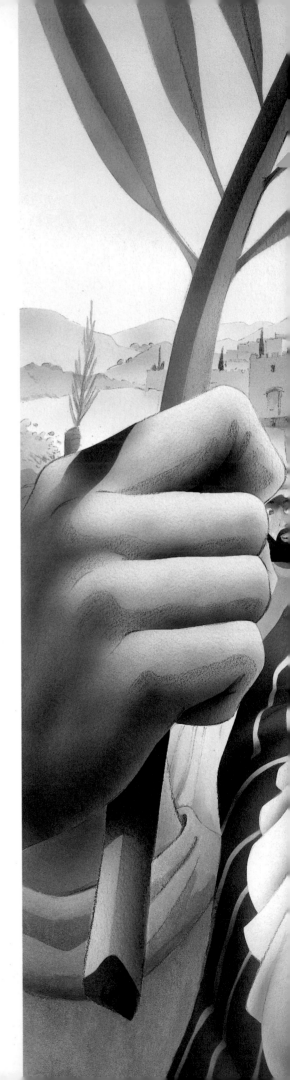

Jesus and his apostles were near to Jerusalem. Jesus sent two apostles to find a donkey and bring it back so that he could ride on it into the city. When Jesus was sitting on the donkey, a great crowd of people followed him.

They cut branches from the trees and spread them on the road in front of Jesus. The apostles rejoiced and praised God with loud voices for all the miracles and mighty works they had seen Jesus do. The crowd shouted, "Hosanna! Blessed is he who comes in the name of the Lord! Hosanna in the highest!"

Followed by the crowd, Jesus entered Jerusalem. The whole city was stirred up and the chief priests complained to Jesus. They wanted him to tell his apostles to be quiet. But Jesus said, "If I told them to be silent, the very stones in the ground would cry out."

(Matthew 21:1–11; Mark 11:1–11; Luke 19:28–40; John 12:12–19)

THE INSTITUTION OF THE HOLY EUCHARIST

Jesus told his apostles that they would celebrate the Passover together for the last time while they were in Jerusalem. He told them that he was going to be betrayed and put to death.

While they were at supper, Jesus took bread into his hands and gave thanks to God. Jesus blessed the bread and broke it. He gave it to his apostles saying, "Take this, all of you, and eat it; for this is my body which will be given up for you."

When supper was ended, Jesus took a chalice of wine. Again, he gave thanks to God. Jesus blessed the chalice and gave it to his apostles saying, "Take this, all of you, and drink from it; for this is the chalice of my blood, the blood of the new and eternal covenant which will be poured out for you and for many for the forgiveness of sins. Do this in memory of me."

(Matthew 20:17–19, 26:17–30; Mark 10:32–34, 14:12–25; Luke 18:31–34, 22:7–23)

THE BETRAYAL

Jesus knew that Judas Iscariot had been tempted by Satan, and had agreed to betray him for thirty pieces of silver. While they were eating, Jesus said to Judas, "What you are going to do, do quickly." Judas got up and went to find soldiers to arrest Jesus.

After the meal, Jesus and his apostles went to pray in the Garden of Gethsemane. Soon, Judas and a band of soldiers arrived. "You should arrest the man I greet with a kiss," he told them. Judas went to Jesus and kissed him. "Judas, would you betray me with a kiss?" Jesus asked him sorrowfully. The other apostles wanted to fight so that Jesus could escape, but he went with the soldiers calmly.

The next morning, Judas said, "I have sinned. Jesus is innocent." But the chief priests would not take back the silver. Judas threw the money to the ground. He did not think his sin could be forgiven and he hanged himself.

(Matthew 26:14–16, 26:36–56, 27:3–10; Mark 14:32–50; Luke 22:1–6, 22:39–53; John 18:1–12)

JESUS BEFORE PILATE

The high council, known as the Sanhedrin, questioned Jesus harshly about his teachings. They asked if he was the Son of God. "It is you who say so," replied Jesus. "But I will say this: One day you will see me sitting at the right hand of God and coming back on the clouds of heaven." With these words, Jesus acknowledged that he was the Son of God.

The council accused Jesus of blasphemy, and took him to the Roman governor, Pontius Pilate. They demanded that Jesus be put to death. Pilate asked Jesus if he was the King of the Jews. Jesus answered, "You have said so."

It was the custom for Pilate to release one prisoner during the Passover. Pilate asked the crowd if they wanted Jesus or a notorious criminal called Barabbas released. "Release Barabbas!" cried the crowd, "Crucify Jesus!" Pilate washed his hands and said, "I am innocent of this man's blood; see to it yourselves." Jesus was led away.

(Matthew 26:57–68, 27:11–26; Mark 14:53–65, 15:1–15; Luke 22:66–71, 23:1–25; John 18:19–24, 18:28–40, 19:1–16)

THE WAY OF THE CROSS

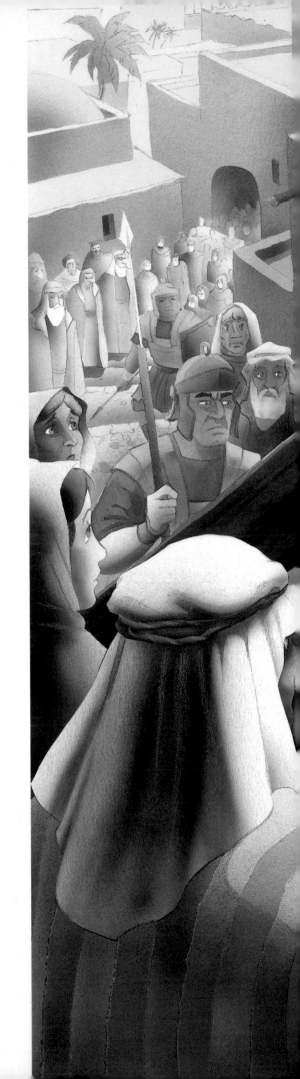

Pontius Pilate's soldiers tied Jesus to a pillar and whipped him. Then they put a scarlet robe over his wounds and pressed a crown of thorns onto his head. "Hail, King of the Jews!" they mocked. Then they continued to beat him with reeds and sticks.

When they were tired, the soldiers put Jesus' own clothes back on him and laid the heavy cross on his back. They made Jesus walk through Jerusalem to Mount Calvary where he was going to be crucified. While they were walking, the soldiers forced a man named Simon of Cyrene to help Jesus carry the cross.

Women in the crowd following Jesus were mourning for him. Jesus stopped and said, "Daughters of Jerusalem, do not weep for me but for your children. For the time will come when people will say to the mountains, 'Fall on us,' and to the hills, 'Cover us.'" In this way Jesus predicted the future destruction of Jerusalem.

(Matthew 27:27–32; Mark 15:16–22; Luke 23:26–31; John 19:16–17)

THE CRUCIFIXION

At the place called Golgotha, the soldiers nailed Jesus to the cross. Two robbers were crucified at the same time. The chief priests came to mock Jesus. "He is the Son of God," they laughed. "And he cannot even save himself!" Jesus prayed, "Father, forgive them for they know not what they do."

The robber next to Jesus rebuked them. He said, "Jesus, remember me when you come into your kingdom." Jesus promised, "Today you will be with me in Paradise." Jesus' mother Mary was near with his apostle John. Jesus said, "Woman, here is your son" and "Son, here is your mother."

As Jesus hung on the cross, he cried out, "My God, my God, why have you forsaken me?" Then he said, "Father, into your hands I commend my spirit," and died. When the soldier pierced Jesus' side with a spear to make sure he was dead, blood and water gushed out. The centurion said, "Truly this was the Son of God."

(Matthew 27:33–56; Mark 15:22–41; Luke 23:33–49; John 19:18–37)

THE RESURRECTION

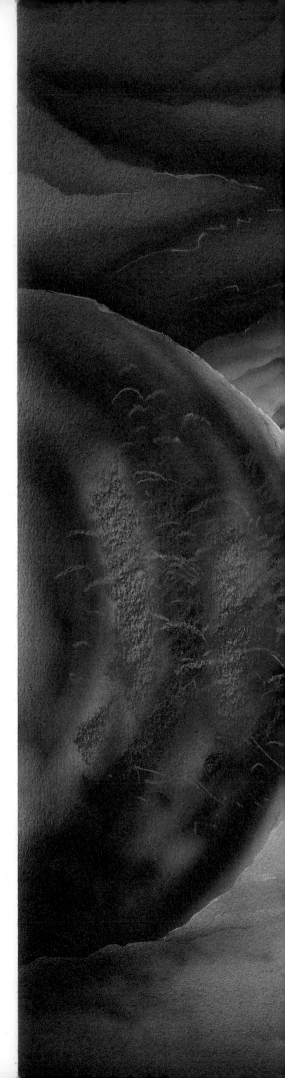

Joseph of Arimathea asked Pontius Pilate for Jesus' body. Joseph and the apostles wrapped Jesus' body with linen and spices, laid it in a tomb, and rolled a huge stone over the entrance.

After three days, Mary Magdalene and two other women went to visit Jesus' tomb. There was a great earthquake and an angel of the Lord descended to roll away the stone. The angel's clothes were as white as snow and his face was like lightning. He said, "Do not be afraid. I know that you are looking for Jesus who was crucified. He is not here. He has risen!"

Joyfully the women ran to tell the apostles. On their way, Jesus met them and said, "Do not be afraid; go and tell my apostles to go to Galilee where they will see me." When the women told the apostles the angel's message, they remembered that Jesus had told them that the Son of God must die and rise again.

(Matthew 27:57–61, 28:1–10; Mark 15:42–47, 16:1–11; Luke 23:50–56, 24:1–12; John 19:38–42, 20:1–18)

THE ROAD TO EMMAUS

Jesus appeared to two of his followers as they were walking to the town of Emmaus. They did not recognize him, but welcomed him as a traveling companion. "Some claim to have seen Jesus risen from the dead," one said, "but that is impossible." Jesus explained how the prophets had foretold that the Son of God would be crucified and rise from the dead. When they stopped for a meal, Jesus took bread and blessed it. He broke it and gave it to them. Then they recognized him at once. But Jesus disappeared.

Later that evening Jesus appeared in the middle of a crowd of disciples. They were afraid and thought he was a ghost. "Peace be with you," Jesus said. "Why do you doubt who I am? Touch me and see the wounds in my hands and feet." Then Jesus ate with them and opened their minds to understand the scriptures which said he had to suffer and rise from the dead for the forgiveness of sins.

(Mark 16:12–14; Luke 24:13–49; John 20:19–29)

THE ASCENSION

The apostles went out to the Mount of Olives, where they had once prayed with Jesus. There he appeared to them for the last time. "All authority in heaven and on earth has been given to me," Jesus said. "Go therefore and make disciples of all nations, baptizing them in the name of the Father, and of the Son, and of the Holy Spirit. Teach everyone to observe all that I have commanded you. I am with you always."

Jesus lifted up his hands and blessed them. At that moment he was taken into heaven where he sits at God's right hand. The apostles worshipped Jesus and returned to Jerusalem with great joy. They did all that he had said they would. In Jesus' name, the apostles preached the gospel, cast out demons, spoke in new languages, and healed the sick. Wherever they traveled many people listened, many believed. And many turned to God, just as Jesus had foretold.

(Matthew 28:16–20; Mark 16:15–20; Luke 24:44–53)